Cats

by **Renee C. Rebman**

Marshall Cavendish
Benchmark
New York

For my sister-in-law, Carolyn Zajack

Thanks to Donald E. Moore III, associate director of animal care at
the Smithsonian Institutions National Zoo, for his expert reading of this manuscript.

Marshall Cavendish Benchmark
99 White Plains Road
Tarrytown, New York 10591-5502
www.marshallcavendish.us

All websites were available and accurate when this book was sent to press.

Library of Congress Cataloging-in-Publication Data

Rebman, Renée C., 1961-
Cats / by Renee C. Rebman.
p. cm. — (Animals animals)
Includes index.
Summary: "Provides comprehensive information on the anatomy, special
skills, habitats, and diet of cats"—Provided by publisher.
ISBN 978-0-7614-3975-2
1. Cats—Juvenile literature. I. Title.
SF445.7.R434 2009
636.8—dc22
2008020918

Photo research by Joan Meisel

Cover photo: Aaron Bean

The photographs in this book are used by permission and through the courtesy of:
AP Images: 36, 41. *Aaron Bean*: 1, 20, 27. *Alamy*: Martin Shields, 7; Arco Images GmbH, 9; blickwinkel, 18;
Mark A. Johnson, 21; TOPICMedia/W. Layer, 32; Andre Jenny, 39. *Animals Animals - Earth Scenes*: Robert Maier, 13;
Gerard Lacz, 16; Henry Ausloos, 23. *Art Resource, NY*: British Museum, 11. *Corbis*: DLILLC, 4; Roy Morsch, 35;
Jerry McCrea/Star Ledger, 38. *Minden Pictures*: Mitsuaki Iwago, 24, 28, 30. *Peter Arnold Inc.*: Biosphoto/Klein J.-L., 33.
Photo Researchers, Inc.: Stephen Dalton, 15; *SuperStock*: age fotostock, 26.

Editor: Joy Bean
Publisher: Michelle Bisson
Art Director: Anahid Hamparian
Series Designer: Adam Mietlowski

Printed in Malaysia
1 3 5 6 4 2

Contents

1 Feline History

A large, striped *tomcat* stretches out in a patch of sun. Suddenly, he lifts his head and turns his pointed ears. He detects a soft rustle. In a flash, he gathers his body into a crouch. Every muscle is tense, but the alert cat does not move an inch. He spies a mouse a few feet away and waits for his chance. In a split second, he pounces and catches the mouse in his front claws. Somebody pulls a string, and the mouse is jerked away. The cat pounces again as he plays with his owner. He is practicing his hunting skills on a toy mouse in the wilds of the family living room. The tomcat is as fierce as a tiger.

(From left) The lion, jaguar, and tiger are part of the same family, Felidae, as the domestic cat.

Cats all belong to the same family—the scientific classification called Felidae. This family includes both small cats and big cats. Lions, tigers, and cheetahs are some of the big cats. Small *domestic* cats belong to the species *Felis catus*.

All cats come from common *prehistoric* ancestors. Catlike animals appeared on the earth around 40 million years ago. These creatures had cutting teeth to tear their food. These *fangs* appeared in prehistoric cats through the ages and evolved to a large size on the best-known prehistoric big cat—the saber-toothed tiger.

Scientists call the saber-toothed tiger Smilodon. Smilodon first appeared about 1.8 million years ago and died out about ten thousand years ago. The La Brea Tar Pits in California have *fossilized* remains of these animals. At one time, the tar pits were sticky pools that trapped animals as they walked through them. Scientists gather information about the ancient animals by studying their fossilized bones.

Scientists think that Smilodon was about 10 feet (3 meters) long and weighed nearly 1,000 pounds (454 kilograms)—twice as much as a lion. Its fangs were over 7 inches (18 centemeters) long.

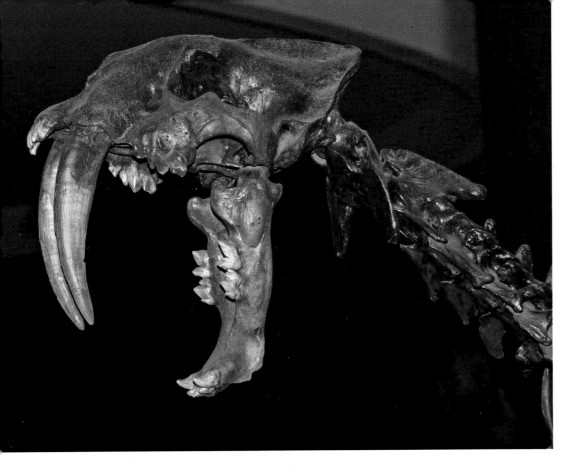

This is a skeleton of the saber-toothed tiger Smilodon, which was pulled from the La Brea Tar Pits. It is on display at the Page Museum in Los Angeles, California.

Humans have lived with cats for over five thousand years. The cats we know as pets are most likely descended from African wildcats. The first known records of household cats come from ancient Egypt and date back to 3500 BCE. By that time, humans had already been keeping dogs, sheep, and cows on their land.

Egyptian paintings show cats drinking from their own bowls and hunting with their masters. People relied on cats to keep rodents out of stored grain.

Species Chart

◆ The largest domestic cat breed is the Maine Coon. The males of the breed weigh 13 to 20 pounds (5.9 to 9.1 kg) and reach 40 inches (102 cm) in length. Maine Coons do not reach their full adult size until they are four to five years old. They have bushy tails and distinctive fur around the chest that resembles a lion's mane. Their soft long fur needs special grooming and the breed is popular in cat shows. It is one of the oldest natural breeds in North America and is the official state cat of Maine.

◆ The Sphynx cat or Canadian Hairless is the most unusual breed. It appears to be hairless but has a soft, nearly invisible peach fuzz covering of downy hairs. Their skin is either solid with markings around the face and paws, or tortoise colored. Sphynx cats have heavy bodies and wedge-shaped heads. Their natural body oils build up on their skin, and they need weekly baths. The Sphynx is strictly an indoor cat and has to stay out of the sun, as it can burn easily. This breed is naturally curious and affectionate and loves to cuddle.

The Sphynx is easily recognizable because of its lack of long fur.

Egyptians loved and honored their cats. When a family's pet cat died, the family went into mourning. They shaved their eyebrows to show their grief. Then they mummified the cat's body and buried it in a pet cemetery. Cats were protected by law in ancient Egypt. Anyone who killed a cat was punished with death.

Egyptians depicted one of their goddesses as a woman who has the head of a cat—or sometimes with the body of a whole cat. She was known as Bastet. Egyptians believed the goddess Bastet was a protector and healer. Some people kept a small statue of her in their homes to protect themselves from robbers, fire, and illness.

As people moved throughout the world, so did cats. Cats were great favorites on sailing ships. They killed rats and kept the sailors company. They were considered good luck. Then, during the Middle Ages (500–1400), people developed *superstitions* about cats. They associated cats with witches and the devil. Many cats, especially black ones, were sent away or killed.

In the 1700s, cats once again became popular as pets. People became interested in exotic *breeds*. For

This statue of Bastet was made of gold and bronze in Egypt around 718 BCE.

Did You Know . . .

For an unknown reason, most white cats with blue eyes are deaf. White cats with other eye colors do not have this disability. If a white cat has one blue eye and one different-colored eye, it is deaf only in the ear closest to the blue eye.

example, the famous cats of Siam (now the country of Thailand), had elegant brown markings. These cats could only be owned by royalty.

The first cat show took place in London in 1871. People showed Siamese and Persian cats along with other breeds. The show was so popular that *pedigreed* breeds were in large demand. People began breeding and showing cats. The first major cat show in the United States was held in New York City in 1881.

The Siamese breed of cats has been popular for hundreds of years.

Today there are about forty breeds of domestic cats. Cats without a pedigree are sometimes known as strays, barn cats, or alley cats. Many people find them just as desirable as pets. It is estimated that 88 million people in the Unites States own cats. About 75 million own dogs. These are only estimates, but they show that people love cats and that they are an important part of people's lives.

2 The Amazing Feline Body

Cats leap, pounce, walk silently, and curl into tight balls of fur to sleep. Their bodies can do many amazing things. Domestic cats are built much like smaller versions of the big cats. Most domestic cats weigh between 6 and 15 pounds (2.7 and 6.8 kg).

A cat's body is made up of 230 bones. (A human being has 206 bones.) Cats owe their *agility* to their flexible skeletal system. It is designed for freedom of movement. Cats' *vertebrae*, the small bones that form the backbone, are more loosely connected than those of humans. This allows cats to curl up, stretch, and twist. Their tailbones are like an extension of their vertebrae. Cats use their tails to stay balanced.

Cats, especially kittens, love to play, and they can leap into the air without any problem.

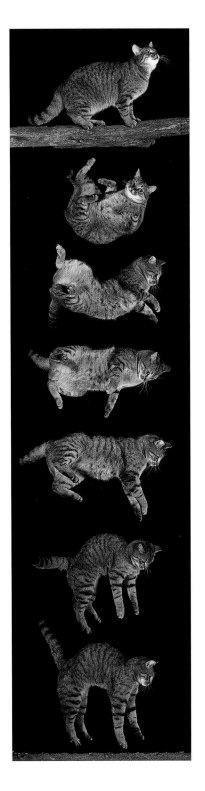

The self-righting reflex can be seen here, in which a cats falls but lands on its feet.

All cats have an amazing characteristic called the *self-righting reflex*. If a cat falls from a high place, it automatically rotates its head and spine, and then aligns its rear legs and arches its back to soften the landing. In other words, cats will almost always land on their feet.

A cat's femur, the large thighbone, is long compared with the size of the entire animal. It is covered by strong, flexible muscle. This allows cats to run very fast and to leap high into the air.

Another unusual part of the feline skeleton is the collarbone. It is not rigid like the human collarbone. The shoulder joint is connected to the collarbone by a very small bone held in place by muscle. A cat can actually bend and twist its shoulders and squeeze through small spaces.

Cats have about twelve whiskers on each side of their upper lips. People generally believe that if a cat can fit its head through a tight space without its whiskers brushing the sides, the rest of its body will fit. While there is no scientific proof that this is a precise measurement, cats do use their whiskers to judge how close an object is and to find their way in the dark.

Very few animals can walk as silently as a cat. Their soft paws have spongy pads of flesh surrounded by fur. Cats actually walk on their toes. This is known as a *digitigrade stride*. Humans walk with a *plantigrade stride*, or with the heal touching the ground. Animals with a digitigrade stride can move faster and make quicker stops and turns. Shifting on a small surface area allows the cat to be much more agile. This is also why tennis players stay on their toes when performing fast moves.

Cats have *retractable* claws. The tough, curved nails are protected by a sheath inside the paws. A cat can extend its claws when it is threatened by a predator or when it needs to make a quick getaway by climbing up a tree.

All cats instinctively scratch their front claws against rough surfaces. This behavior is called stropping. Stropping keeps claws sharp and removes old, peeling outer layers. Cats chew off the dead layers of

Outdoor cats usually sharpen their claws on trees, but indoor cats can use a scratching post to achieve the same results.

their back claws. The stropping instinct is so deeply ingrained that even house cats with their claws removed continue to strop.

The soft fur of a cat consists of three layers. The undercoat of short, fine fur is called down hairs. Slightly longer and more bristly awn hairs make up the middle coat. The top coat is made of guard hairs, which are longer. The guard hairs define the look of a cat. For example, the guard hairs on a long-haired breed such as the Persian can grow to 5 inches (12.7 cm) in length.

Another distinctive feline feature is their almond-shaped eyes. Cats have very good eyesight and need only one-sixth the amount of light to see that a human does. Their *irises* open widely to let in a lot of light in dim light, and narrow to slits in very bright light. At the back of a cat's eye is a special layer of tissue known as the tapetum lucidum. This layer collects and reflects light to help the cat see. It also gives cats' eyes their mysterious glow.

A cat's sense of hearing is also highly developed. Cats can hear sounds at very high frequencies, such as the high-pitched squeaking of a mouse. They can turn just one ear, or both, in order to catch sounds.

Did You Know . . .

A cat's nose has 19 million nerve endings that give it a sharp sense of smell. Human noses have about 5 million nerve endings. Cats use their noses to explore new spaces and to identify people, food, possible mates, and their own familiar territory. Every cat's nose has a unique pattern of ridges, just as human fingerprints are unique to each individual.

A cat's eyes are large compared with the size of its body. Cats have very good eyesight, both in light and in dark.

These characteristics help make them skilled hunters.

Cats have an unusual organ in the roofs of their mouths. It is called the *Jacobsen's* or *vomeronasal organ*. This special gland

20

allows the animal to taste scent particles. In order to do this, the cat curls back its lips and draws in air through its open mouth. This behavior is known as *flehmen breathing*. Cats seem to use this ability to investigate a new environment or odor.

The fascinating feline body serves the cat well and proves there is nothing at all common about the common house cat.

A cat's sense of smell is fourteen times stronger than that of humans.

3 The Life Cycle of a Cat

Cats are prolific animals. That means they can give birth to many offspring over the course of their lifetimes. Cats can have their first *litter* of kittens at a young age, from six to nine months old. They can produce two litters a year. Cats can continue to have kittens until they are around twelve years old.

A female who is ready to mate is called a queen. A male is called a tom. During mating season, a queen may mate with more than one tom. She can become pregnant each time she mates. Her kittens may well have different fathers even though they are from the same litter.

A queen has a *gestation* period of around sixty-five days. While she is waiting to give birth, she looks

A mother nurses her kittens so they can grow up big and strong.

for a nest site. A house cat may prefer the dark corner of a closet. An outside or *feral* (wild) cat will search out a shed or perhaps a dry, quiet area under a porch. The mother cat is looking for privacy and safety. As her birthing time becomes closer, she may become anxious or restless and she may lose her appetite.

Once the birthing process begins, the first kitten arrives in about thirty minutes. Kittens are born fifteen to thirty minutes apart. Most queens have four or more kittens per litter. The mother cat uses her rough tongue to lick her newborn kittens clean. Kittens are born blind and nearly deaf. They are totally helpless. Instinct drives them to begin to nurse.

When kittens are newly born, their eyes are sealed shut, so they are blind until they are two to three weeks old.

The kittens snuggle under their mother's belly and begin to suckle. Once they find a spot to nurse from, the kittens come back to the same spot each time they nurse. As they nurse, they continually press their paws into their mother. This instinctive kneading action helps the mother's milk to flow. Her milk has *nutrients* that the kittens need, and it also helps prevent disease.

Kittens weigh 2 to 5 ounces (57 to 142 grams) when they are born. They grow quickly, and at eight days they begin to open their eyes. At about two to three weeks they can see and hear. Around three or four weeks of age, they may begin to eat solid food, although they still need mother's milk until about six to eight weeks old. After four months they do not need their mother at all. Humans may take a kitten away from its mother and into its new home as early as six weeks of age.

Kittens soon begin to play with their brothers and sisters. Pouncing, chasing, wrestling, and jumping help the kittens develop physically, mentally, and socially. They learn to climb trees, stalk prey, and

Did You Know . . .
Cats carry their kittens by the scruff of the neck. This might look painful, but it does not hurt the kitten at all. Kittens have a reflex that automatically stops them from moving when they are grabbed. The mother cat then has a firm hold on the still kitten and can transport it safely.

capture small animals. These survival skills are necessary for feral and outdoor cats. Indoor pets do not need these skills to survive, but such play enriches their lives. Pet cats continue to play long into adulthood, especially if their owners encourage them.

Some cat experts think that five months of age marks the end of childhood for a cat. This means that cats live many years as adults. Feral cats and outdoor pets are exposed to a wide range of dangers—other animals that can harm them or spread disease, bad weather, and automobiles. If they are lucky, they live to be around ten years old. Indoor pets that have proper care may live sixteen years or longer. A ten-year-old cat is equal to a human of about sixty years old.

Old age can bring problems for cats. They can get some of the same diseases as humans, such as diabetes and kidney failure. Older cats may also suffer loss of hearing or sight. They can become nervous, especially about loud noises or any changes in their environment. Older cats tend to lead quiet lives, and they sleep even more than younger cats. Pet owners need to be especially sensitive to their needs. No matter what their age, all cats need care and love.

Older cats, such as this fourteen-year-old female, may sleep more than younger cats, but she can lead a happy, healthy life with regular veterinarian checkups.

4 Cat Behaviors

All cats purr, hiss, and arch their backs. What do these behaviors mean? They are simply ways to communicate, just like a cat's meow. Each unique cat behavior has a meaning. Some behaviors are driven by physical needs. Some characteristics are just part of being a cat.

All cats, and many humans, take catnaps. Cats can fall into a deep sleep almost any time of the day or night. These naps may last from a few minutes to several hours. Cats sleep as much as sixteen hours per day. This is much more time than other animals spend, and there is no known cause for this behavior.

When frightened or threatened, cats will puff up in order to look larger to their enemy.

Cats are most alert at dawn and dusk because these times are better for hunting. Even house cats that have never hunted real prey follow this pattern.

Cats are self-cleaning animals. They *groom* themselves every day. Felines use their rough tongues and moist *saliva* to scrub their coats and to keep them shiny and free of dirt. Because cats are incredibly

A cat's tongue is rough, perfect for grooming its fur.

flexible, they can reach every part of their body except their head and face. Cats lick their paws and rub them over these areas to clean them.

Grooming also helps calm a cat. Cats often groom if they are under stress. If a cat is upset or even bored for long periods of time, it might groom itself to the point of causing bald spots on its body. When a cat grooms, it eats small amounts of fur that it coughs up later as a fur ball.

Cats are territorial animals. They mark their territory by spraying urine. A cat can smell another cat's markings and can even tell how fresh they are. Indoor pets trained to use a litter box usually do not spray their territory unless they are stressed. For example, if another animal is introduced into the household, a previously litter-trained cat might begin to spray. A house cat also marks its territory with scent glands in the sides of its face. This is why cats rub their jaws against furniture, walls, and even people. Cats also bump heads when they greet each other or humans they like. Bumping heads is a sign of acceptance and affection.

Angry cats hiss. This is an unmistakable warning to keep away. A cat facing a threat will arch its back

When a cat is angry, it will hiss at its enemy to warn it to stay away.

to make itself appear larger. Its fur will bristle and puff out. An aggressive cat stares directly at an opponent and rotates its ears. All these signs mean the cat is better left alone.

A cat that is nervous or shy crouches down and tries to make itself appear smaller. It also flattens its ears against its head. A crouched, quiet cat is showing *submission*, but the cat is still ready to spring into action and defend itself in a split second if it is attacked or threatened.

A happy, friendly cat walks in a relaxed manner with its tail raised. It may greet a human with any number of friendly noises, such as a chirp or a gentle meow. More than twenty distinct cat sounds have been documented. Each sound is a form of communication. With a little practice, cat owners can understand these sounds. For example, the demanding yowl of a hungry cat can hardly be mistaken.

Did You Know . . .

The kneading instinct in cats never goes away. When a cat touches soft material, such as a blanket, it often instinctively begins to knead the material with its paws. Cats even knead their human companions. For example, when sitting on a person's lap, a cat will knead his or her legs. Some animal experts find that this action soothes the cat.

This cat is communicating happiness to its owner by bumping its head against her.

Kittens are very curious creatures and their curiosity sometimes gets them into trouble.

One unique feline sound is the purr. All cats, even the big cats, purr. Scientists think that mother cats use this form of communication to comfort their kittens. Perhaps this is why cats purr when being petted or groomed. A content cat almost always purrs—but cats also purr when they are in pain, sick, or fearful. Cat experts believe purring is caused by vibrations in a cat's vocal cords and diaphragm (the muscle used to breathe).

Cats can be mysterious creatures. They are loving pets, but they are also very independent. Their behaviors are fascinating to watch and can be understood with experience. Feline ways may be frustrating to humans but are part of a cat's charm.

5 A Part of Our World

Human owners take care of millions of cats around the world. Unfortunately, millions more cats have no owners to take care of them. Overpopulation of cats is a huge problem, and irresponsible owners make it worse. Some owners' cats have litters of unwanted kittens, which are sometimes taken from their mothers and abandoned. Other owners simply stop taking care of their pets, and they become strays. Sometimes owners try to care for too many cats, and the cats do not get enough food or proper medical attention. There are ways to deal with this problem.

Owners who do not want their cats to breed can have a veterinarian spay or neuter the cats. Spaying

These kittens were born to a stray mother cat, and they are now hoping to be adopted from the animal shelter where they are being cared for.

(for females) and neutering (for males) are medical procedures that make the animals unable to have kittens. These procedures are extremely important in preventing further overpopulation of cats.

Abandoned pets are only part of the problem. Feral cats number in the millions. There are perhaps as many, or more, feral cats than domestic cats. Feral cats grow up without human contact. They are often the second or third generation of abandoned cats. These cats quickly return to a wild state and view

These adult cats spend their days in their kennels at an animal shelter in New Jersey. They are looking for someone to adopt them.

people as dangerous. The majority of feral cats cannot be tamed or taken in as pets.

While cats are generally independent animals and do not seek out other cats for companionship, feral cats often live in colonies. A colony inhabits in a specific area such as near a restaurant dumpster, alley, or abandoned building. These tough cats live where food is available or where people leave food out for them. Colony life represents safety, and the cats trust each other. Colony members are hostile to cats outside of the colony whether they are feral cats or pets. Some feral females will even nurse and raise *orphaned* feral kittens within the colony. Still, because of poor living conditions and malnutrition, more than half the kittens born within a colony will die.

These feral cats will spend their lives together in a group, looking for food where they can.

Feral colonies can cause problems for humans who live nearby. Toms protecting their territory may fight other cats. Combat over females also occurs frequently, and the noise can be very loud. Cats marking their territory leave terrible odors. Sick animals spread diseases to others in the colony or to any pets that come in contact with them. Feral cats often get infected with *rabies*. This disease is spread to humans through saliva and can be deadly.

All cats, even domestic pets, have *predatory* instincts. Feral cats use these instincts to survive. They hunt mice, rabbits, squirrels, and birds. Some experts claim feral cats are causing a decline in the population of songbirds and other wildlife in certain areas. People argue about the proper solution.

Animal shelters do not have the money or staff to remove feral cats. Even when entire colonies are removed, new colonies move into desirable areas almost immediately.

Another way to address overpopulation is through special groups that work specifically with feral cats and promote Trap-Neuter-Return (TNR). With this method, feral cats are safely trapped and then treated by veterinarians. The cats are spayed or neutered

Demonstrators push for a Trap-Neuter-Return policy to be passed in Florida.

and vaccinated against rabies. The cats also have one ear surgically clipped or "tipped" as it is commonly called. This means the point of the ear is safely cut off to identify that the animal has been spayed or neutered. The treated cats are then returned to their colony. The goal is for all cats within the colony to be trapped, neutered, and returned. This method leaves a healthier colony that will *stabilize* in number rather than growing out of control.

Humans can help fix the problems that face the species. Responsible pet ownership is essential. These fascinating animals deserve proper care and love. Cats need help from humans in order to live better lives. And there is no doubt that many humans have better lives because of cats.

Glossary

agility—The ability to move quickly, easily, and gracefully.

breeds—Specific types of animals within the same species.

digitigrade stride—A stride in which an animal walks on its toes.

domestic—Suitable for living and working with humans.

fangs—Long, sharp teeth.

feral—Having escaped from domestication and turned wild.

flehmen breathing—The lip curl response to odor that allows a cat to draw scent particles into its mouth.

fossilized—Remains of plants or animals preserved in the earth.

gestation—The time when an animal is pregnant.

groom—To make clean and neat.

Jacobsen's organ (vomeronasal organ)—An organ on the roof of a cat's mouth that is used for tasting and smelling.

irises—Dark portions of the center of the eye that regulate the amount of light that enters the eyeball.

litter—A group of kittens that a mother cat gives birth to at the same time.

nutrients—Healthful, nourishing substances such as vitamins and proteins.

orphaned—Having no remaining parents.

pedigreed—Belonging to a breed with a record-ed line of ancestors.

plantigrade stride—Walking on the soles of feet.

predatory—Preying on other animals.

prehistoric—Existing before written history began.

rabies—A deadly viral disease spread by the saliva of an infected animal.

retractable—Capable of being drawn back in.

saliva—A liquid secreted in the mouth that helps digestion.

self-righting reflex—The twisting motion that allows a cat always to land on its feet.

stabilize—To keep steady.

stropping—Dragging claws over a rough surface.

submission—Surrender to a more powerful individual or force.

superstitions—Beliefs that often involve magic or unproven legends.

tomcat—An adult male cat.

vertebrae—The bones that make up the backbone or spine.

Find Out More

Books

Bozzo, Linda. *My First Cat*. Berkeley Heights, NJ: Enslow Publishers, 2008.

Comte, Hubert. *Cats*. New York: Harry N. Abrams, 2005.

Singer, Marilyn. *Cats to the Rescue*. New York: Henry Holt and Company, 2006.

Web Sites

American Society for the Prevention of Cruelty to Animals
www.aspca.org

Cat Site
www.thecatsite.com

Humane Society of the United States
www.hsus.org

The International Cat Association
www.tica.org

Index

Page numbers for illustrations are in **boldface**.

About the Author

Renee C. Rebman has published more than a dozen nonfiction books for young readers. Her Marshall Cavendish titles include *Anteaters, Turtles and Tortoises,* and *Cows.* She is also a published playwright. Her plays have been produced in schools and community theaters across the country. She lives with a black cat named Jezebel.